Roger Coote and Diana Bentley

My Garden

Peter, Mary, Elizabeth and John are friends.

5

Mary lives in a large house with a very big garden.

Mary's grandfather lives there too. He likes to walk around the garden and look at all the flowers. He makes sure they have enough water to help them grow.

John, Elizabeth and
Peter have come to
visit Mary and
her grandfather to
see their garden.

Mary's grandfather shows them
the roses and the daisies ...

... and the fruit trees.
There are apple trees,
cherry trees and
pear trees too.

In the pond there are
lots of goldfish.
They like to hide under the
beautiful water-lilies.

Mary's grandfather takes them all
into the greenhouse.

The greenhouse keeps the flowers and plants warm so that they grow faster.

Mary's grandfather tells the friends how plants grow.
'These are daisy seeds ...

… if you put a seed in a flower pot, after a few days the seed sends out some small roots …

and after a few more days
it starts to grow into a small plant
and then …

… when it has grown bigger
it can be put in a bigger flower pot
and watered until …

... lots of flowers appear.'

'I'm glad you came to
see my garden' said Mary.
'Now let's go and play.'

Notes for adults

Children who come to school already knowing how a book 'works' have a great deal of knowledge that will help them to make the entry into reading much easier. It is far more important to share a book with a child than to try to teach him/her to read. These books aim to introduce very young children to the world around them.

Before reading this book talk about the pictures on the cover. What does your child think the book is about? Talk about the title and point to the words. Tell him/her that all books are written by authors and often illustrated by a different person. Show them the names of the author and illustrator.

Before reading the story look through the book together and talk about the illustrations. Encourage your child to tell his/her own story to the pictures. This important pre-reading skill helps children to develop an understanding of story that is essential to reading.

Do let your child hold the book and give him/her time to look at the pictures before talking about them. Adults often rush in with questions far too soon.

REMEMBER when looking at the pictures there is no 'right' or 'wrong' guess. Accept what your child suggests and add your own ideas. You will be bringing much more knowledge to the pictures but s/he may surprise you.

After reading the book let your child explore the book on his/her own. S/he may want to return to a favourite picture, retell the story to a special toy, or just turn the pages pretending to be a reader. A joy in books comes from being allowed to use them as the reader wishes and not necessarily as a parent would have them do.

Discussion points

Talking about the illustrations will help your child to get more from the story. Here are some suggestions for things to discuss. The numbers refer to the pages on which the illustrations appear.

5	What are the friends playing? Can you do this?
7	May lives in this house. Can you guess which is her bedroom window?
9	What do you think Mary's Grandfather is looking at? How many different kinds of trees can you find?
12/13	Can you find five different kinds of flowers? What colours are they?
15	Why is Mary running? What does Peter want to eat?
17	What can Peter see?
19	Can you see the birds? Do you think they will get inside the greenhouse?
21	What is Peter touching? Will he like it?
24/25	What is happening in these pictures?
26/27	Why does he take the plant out of the pot? Why do you think it has to have water?